FANCY A CUPPA?

The Hilarious Guide to British Slang

Jeff Watson

Table of Contents

Chapter One

INTRODUCTION

"Sir, you are drunk."

"Well, perhaps I am rather drunk tonight, but in the morning I shall be sober; and you will still be ugly."

Winston Churchill

Two nations separated by a common language. We all know what that means, don't we? English. The language of the world, spoken officially by 67 countries and a further 27 non-sovereign entities. Everyone knows it, and in the United States, they've embraced it for centuries, but ask an American to walk through the streets of south London, Birmingham, Glasgow and Newcastle, and they may as well try to understand Klingon.

Ahhh, English. A language invented by the English (the clue is in the name…), even if that isn't strictly true as the language came from Germanic, but no one cares about that. Not in this book anyway. It's a language that's become more or less universal, and one that a lot of people now understand, except for when they come to the United Kingdom, because we

British have our own unique way of speaking the language that we gave to the world, and we're going to keep it a secret. Now is your chance to discover that secret...

How to speak British

So what's so unique about *British* English? Well, there are some phrases that have changed over the years, yet somehow mean the same. For instance, we (us Brits) say '**I couldn't care less...**', whilst the Americans say 'I couldn't care more...'. (If you want to sound really British, you could say '**I couldn't give a monkeys...**').

Why the great people of the USA decided to replace the last word is a mystery that no one is bothered about. We say 'do the maths' (because the full word is mathematics, right?), but in the US they say 'math...' Why? No idea...

Words change their meanings and their sounds over time. 'Route' and 'Inquiry' are two words that mean the exact same thing but sound completely different on the opposite sides of the pond. Likewise, descriptions of exactly the same thing have different words.

Pavement/sidewalk, trousers/pants, rubbish/garbage, aeroplane/airplane, car boot/car trunk/ motorway/freeway, mobile phone/cell phone etc etc etc. Oh, and let's not get into the fag, fanny or butt just yet...

The point is, the two countries may as well have completely separate languages, yet somehow, we understand each other. It might not be the case though if you are visiting the United Kingdom of Great Britain and Northern Ireland for the first time. This is where we can help you. This is the interesting part. Read on and learn the lingo. You're in for a treat!

Chapter Two

EMOTIONS AND FEELINGS

"The smell nearly distracted me from my task, but no-I remained steadfast. Stiff upper lip, Watson! Action! Answers!

THEN bacon."

G.S. Denning, *The Hell-Hound of the Baskervilles*

Despite the popular myth that British people don't show their feelings, they do, albeit in a far more reserved way. They don't whoop and holler, they don't cry and weep in public (not often…) and their show of love and affection is usually behind closed doors. Let's look at the expressions that prove that deep down the British do in fact have a heart…

Over the moon – Not used as often now, as it was the preserve of the football (soccer) manager or player twenty years ago, who had just seen his team win a game! It means they are happy. Overjoyed. If someone asks a Brit how they are feeling, and they reply: 'I'm over the moon', then you know they have either had a good day or if they have mastered the art of space-travel. Or they are just being sarcastic… which makes up 99% of British humour. It originated from Ireland in the 18th century and came from a quote unattributed that said the author was so happy, 'he could jump over the moon'.

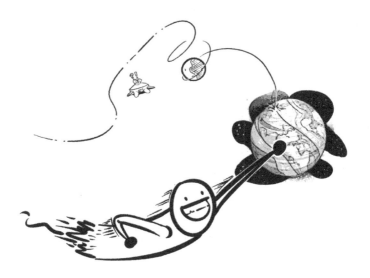

Gobsmacked - This odd word is still used today, even though it came from the counties of Yorkshire and Lincolnshire from so long ago, that nobody is bothered anymore. It means that they are stunned or shocked by an event. If you suddenly opened your front door and a polar bear was stood, drinking a cup of tea and reading the newspaper, you would be 'gobsmacked'! A feeling of being smacked in the gob…your gob, by the way, is your mouth.

As happy as Larry – Ecstatic. 'Over the moon'. Jubilant. Why Larry? Boxer Larry Foley who won a tournament in the 1890s in New Zealand. The newspaper article headline was…?

Befuddled – Totally confused. **Flummoxed**. No idea what is happening.

Gutted – Upset about something. Nearly always spoken by football players after a defeat.

Chuffed – The same as 'happy as Larry' really, except not quite as ecstatic. There is absolutely no explanation whatsoever as to why this word exists.

Not my cup of tea - This is just about the most British saying in a galaxy of British sayings. If a Brit doesn't like something, they won't just say that it's nice, but 'it's not my cup of tea'. It started as 'my cup of tea', which meant they enjoyed it. Obviously, there has to be a negative (in case you haven't noticed yet, the British are very pessimistic…)

Under the Weather – Bearing in mind the British obsession with the weather (of which we will learn in a later chapter), this saying is perfect. It means that the person isn't feeling too well. So instead of saying, 'I've got the flu, I've vomited twelve times this morning, I've got diarrhoea and I feel like dying', the Brit will understate that with 'I'm a little under the weather'. Its origin? From sailors, who when they felt ill, would go below deck to protect themselves from the weather. The Royal Navy's influence is still there today.

Miffed – A bit annoyed. Not really 'angry' annoyed, but more like you are just a tad disappointed.

You're having a laugh!! – This definitely doesn't mean that the person it is spoken to is actually laughing. It's the total opposite. It is the kind of expression that is used when the car mechanic gives you a bill for £500 for replacing a headlight bulb. 'How much? You're having a laugh mate...'. There doesn't appear to be an origin for it, but at a guess, it probably came from the man whose horse needed a new shoe, and the blacksmith said it would be ready next Wednesday and it will cost half of the man's inheritance. That is a guess by the way...

Go spare – Lose your temper. I mean REALLY lose your temper. It comes from being made unemployed in the 1940s. Doesn't mean that anymore.

You might 'go spare' when **'shit hits the fan'** (causing a right old mess!), or everything goes **'pear-shape'**. Basically, when everything going wrong, causing a right old **'shit show'**.

Pissed off – Now this is quintessentially British. It's when you are so very annoyed with a particular situation that you say: 'I'm really pissed off now'. Nothing to do with drink, alcohol or anything that makes you inebriated. It's to do with anger. So, if you want to sound British when you're angry, don't just say 'I'm pissed', but add that little small word 'off' at the end and everyone will know that you're not **mucking around**... (or **'pissing around'**).

Throwing a wobbly – You're having a tantrum. It comes from being 'mentally unbalanced', but thankfully that's not a connection that's made anymore.

Cream crackered – **Knackered**. Knackered? It used to be a sexual term, and also horses who went to the 'knacker's yard', but now it just means tired. Cream crackered is for those trying to be funny.

Float my Boat – This one came from America. It means that something excites or appeals to you (often sexually). Now tell us Brits why we use it more??

Look like death – This one is pretty straight forward. You don't look great! Are you sick?

Daft – Stupid, but quite light. Almost playful.

Buzzin' – Basically, you are extremely excited, usually after your favourite football team wins.

At a loose end – I've got nothing to do. I'm bored and have time. Like a lot of British sayings, it comes from the Navy. When there was nothing to do, the captain would get the sailors to check the loose ends of the rigging. We are a seafaring nation, remember?

Not too bad – Similar to 'under the weather', but is generally positive, meaning you are ok. 'How are you feeling?' 'Not too bad…'. End of conversation.

His ears are burning – Not literally of course, because that would be a little odd. It means someone is talking about them. Their ears then go red. Why? Ask the Romans. They first used the expression in 78BC!

Tickety-boo - I'm fine. I'm okay. All is good. Comes from Scotland originally, so might be worth asking a Scot next time you see one. Another way of saying it would be that everything is **'hunky-dory'**. We like to use that one a lot. It's much more current than 'tickety-boo', which is now reserved for the aging, and those trying to be funny…

Lost the plot – The same as 'off your rocker', 'mad as a hatter', 'bonkers', 'nutter'. What does it mean? You have become a complete withering wreck and can't be helped. Not now anyway.

Full of beans – Nothing to do with flatulence. It means you have lots of energy. Apparently, horses were fed beans to make them run faster. It was never proven though.

Whinge – There are two things that Brits do the best. One is queuing in a line, and the second is whinging. It means moaning and complaining. It comes from a completely unpronounceable word from the Middle Ages, so let's not bother. Let's just have a good whinge instead.

Can't be arsed - I honestly **cannot be bothered**. Nowhere near as polite though.

Bright as a Button – This is used more to describe someone's character, meaning they are very sharp, intelligent, lively, full of energy.

I feel like a million pounds – This means that you are feeling very healthy and happy, or that you look especially great, usually because you are wearing an expensive suit or clothes.

Of course, the Americans have their own version of this saying, replacing 'pounds' with 'dollars' or 'bucks'. You can look forward to British slang terms for money in chapter nine.

Chapter Three

DOWN THE PUB

"A good local pub has much in common with a church, except that a pub is warmer, and there's more conversation."

William Blake

The favourite activity of any Brit has to be 'going down to the pub'. There isn't another country anywhere in the world that has such a culture. Yes, beer is drunk excessively in places like Germany, Australia and Holland, but they don't have the traditional public house, sawdust on the floor (although Health and Safety laws appear to have put a stop to that), juke box in the corner and warm beer served by a buxom barmaid. Utterly British.

Of course, there are all kinds of slang sayings associated with the pub and the activities involved, but here are just a few of the hilarious sayings you might hear, once you've managed to get to the bar and you're now **'On the Lash!'** (in the process of getting drunk…)

Fancy a pint? – This doesn't mean, '**do you fancy**' (like or desire) something that is in, or called, a pint. It means 'do you want to go to the pub and have some beer with me?'. That of course is far too long to say, and most people will stop listening halfway through, so 'fancy a pint?' is the accepted version. Oh, and it's still 'pints' in the UK. None of this litre nonsense.

Watering hole – Just another name for the pub, except a little cleverer.

Mate – The same as a 'geezer' or a 'bloke'. The friends you spend hours with drinking copious amounts of beer.

Girl, hottie, chick, love, darling, babe – All the names and expressions that are guaranteed to get a man a slap around the face when asking the female for a date, especially after a few pints.

Your round – Don't be offended by this. It doesn't mean that the person saying it thinks that your figure is round (and that would be 'you're' anyway), it means it's time for you to buy the group some drinks, as they have been buying them for you all evening. Brace yourself. It will be expensive.

It has great grub though… – Grub means food. That's it. The origin has something to do with the grub insect and digging for food. That's as far as I can go.

Have one on me – Could be open to all kinds of interpretations, except in a pub. It means have a drink with me, to the barman or the barmaid. They won't, because they'll end up as drunk as you, but they will put a few coins in the tip jar to be shared around later.

Pissed – Ok, so when Americans use the word 'pissed' it's because they're pretty damned angry with someone or something. 'I'm pissed about this' is self-explanatory for the English speakers on the other side of the pond, but in the United Kingdom, where the expression originated, it means something ENTIRELY different. If you are 'pissed' in Britain, it's because you are **blind drunk**, helplessly inebriated, **drunk as a skunk** (which is another expression that demands an explanation), **off your head**…It goes on. You'll hear this a lot in a British pub. It means drunk. You've had far too much alcohol and it's the only word that can come close to explaining it…

To continue the theme of being very drunk in a pub, you might also hear the words **'bladdered'**, **'off his face'**, **'out of it'** and **'hammered'**. All of them referring to the inebriated state of the drinker.

On the pull – This is the drunken expression for the male who is looking to find a female for a night of unbridled sex. They go to the pub and drink lots and then use the expressions mentioned earlier. It hardly ever works.

Chunder – **To throw up**, or to vomit. Always after too many beers. It's originally an Australian navy expression, which shows we Brits have no problems stealing other people's ideas (colonialization, baby!)

See a Man about a Dog – By far and away the strangest expression you will ever hear from a Brit, especially in the pub. You might want to ask, who is the man? And where is the dog? There is no man, and there is no dog… It means he's going to the toilet (or somewhere else to do some secret business), but he doesn't really want you to know that, because he's British and polite. Work that one out if you can.

Last orders please! – This is usually accompanied by the ringing of a bell. It means that you have exactly twenty minutes to drink up and get out. The pub is closing, and only those who know the landlord and are very good friends with him, can stay beyond those twenty minutes. This is when the bar becomes at its busiest all evening.

Cheers! – Not the old American sitcom, but a greeting to wish you health and happiness. Came from the 13th century, but now is only used with a pint of beer in your hand. Cheers to what exactly? Nothing in particular…

A night on the town – The same as **'paint the town red'**. It means that you are all going out and visiting every single pub in the area where you can get blind drink. Huntsmen in the past, who had killed quite a few animals, would get drunk and then paint the town red with the blood of their kills. That doesn't happen anymore.

NOW THAT'S FINISHED, LET'S GO PAINT THE TOWN BLUE!

Snog – The most any self-respecting drunken Brit can hope for when 'on the pull' is a snog. It means a kiss. A passionate kiss. See chapter ten…

How to can survive a night on the town with an Englishman.

At this point, you could maybe use a few tips on how to survive a night out with an Englishman. Well, listen close.

1. Take a lot of money with you.
2. Drink beer. From the tap if possible. Not the girly-lager stuff. Prepare for ale and bitter and mild. You'll hate the taste but drink it anyway.
3. Have a story to hand about some girl you 'pulled' recently. Don't worry if it's not true, as the story they will tell you won't be either.
4. Know about football. No, not the NFL, but what you might call soccer. Have an opinion on every manager in the English game (or Scottish if you find yourself north of the border).
5. Don't mention religion ever.
6. Don't talk politics ever
7. Make sure you have enough room in your stomach for a greasy kebab at the end of the night. If you don't know what one is, be pleasantly surprised.
8. Don't become awkward when the person you are drinking with starts to become affectionate. It's the beer that is talking, not them.
9. Don't sit at a table and wait to be served. You'll be there all night.
10. Don't order a soft drink.

Chapter Four

WEATHER. The Brits' favourite obsession.

"English rain feels obligatory, like paperwork."

Maureen Johnson

The weather. Along with queueing, apologising, and drinking tea, the other major fascination for Brits is the weather. Is it raining, or has it dried out, or have we seen the sun today? 'We had our summer last week' is a typical way of saying that it's no longer remotely warm. It comes about because the UK is just about the wettest place on the planet.

You can get all four seasons in one afternoon, so the British have always got one eye on the clouds that are permanently above, just waiting to open up and drench us all when we least expect it.

For as long as the United Kingdom exists, the weather will always be a topic of conversation for us Brits. After all, what else could replace the awkward small talk that occurs when you're greeted by someone that you vaguely remember?

Pissing it down – Raining – of course – but not just raining, but **'cats and dogs'** raining. Pissing it down is pretty obvious, but 'cats and dogs' is almost unexplainable, but I'll try.

It comes from the Greek saying 'cata doxa', which means waterfall. We Anglicised it to cats and dogs, which sounds far better.

The heavens opened – Pissing it down

It's chucking it down – Pissing it down still. We can also say it's **'bucketing it down'**, or it's **'raining buckets'**.

Baking hot – Usually said when the temperature gets to about 21 degrees Celsius, or for you Americans, about 70 degrees Fahrenheit. Rarely is it baking in the UK…

Miserable weather – There is never a 'happy weather'. It's always miserable. Almost always refers to the rain – pissing it down!

Freezing - Snow and ice weather. Pour a kettle of hot water over the windscreen in the morning type weather. The kind that stops the trains from running, although there can be many reasons for that.

I'm drenched – You've been caught in the rain without a hat or an umbrella and are very wet. Drenched makes it seem far more dramatic.

Chapter Five

TEA TIME!

"Can I offer you some tea while you ransack our place?' Lockwood asked politely."

Jonathan Stroud

Yes, it's true. The British love tea. They may no longer drink the stuff as much as they used to, but any excuse to stop what they are doing to sit down and have a cuppa is fine by them.

The 'tea break' at work, means just that. Take a break and have some tea. Even in cricket, that gentlest of English sports (and to you Americans the most incomprehensible), there is 'tea', which means the second break of play for the day, usually around 5pm. Tea. We love it!

Fancy a cuppa? – The same as 'fancy a pint?' but not spoken in a pub. A cuppa is the one thing that binds people, so that all the world's problems can be solved over a cup of tea. It's about the most British phrase ever. Hence, it's the title of this book.

Put the kettle on – It doesn't mean to try to put a kettle on your body, but put it on the hob, gas ring or electric plate. More common now is just to switch it on at the mains and wait for the water to boil. There is no more satisfying sound than a kettle that whistles as it boils.

Let's have a natter… - Always at a kitchen table with a strong cup of tea. Natter? It's a chat, a talk, a discussion. Comes from the north of England and means incessant chatter.

Tea-time - In the south of England there's 'lunch' and 'dinner', usually taken at about noon and 5pm respectively. In the north of England, there's 'dinner' and 'tea', usually taken at noon and 5pm respectively. Never confuse these terms!

All the tea in China – If someone says that they won't part with a certain treasured item for 'all the tea in China', it means you have absolutely no chance of getting it, no matter what you offer. Originally an Australian saying, but now it belongs to the British.

Tearoom – They still exist. Used to be very popular in the early part of the 20th century, and now making a comeback. Not just tea, but they serve coffee too!

Teasmade – A curious British contraption that found its way into boarding houses and bed and breakfast establishments in the 1970s. It basically made a pot of tea whilst you were sleeping and was ready for when you woke. Disappeared at the same time as the electric blanket.

Chapter Six

WHAT YOU WEARING?

"Britain: the land of embarrassment and breakfast."

Julian Barnes

If you are a female and planning a night out with the girls, then it seems to be essential that you all agree on what you are going to wear that night. Even though we all want to be individual, it's far better to be part of a crowd and not attract attention. Don't you agree?

Hence the phrase of 'what you wearing?' is probably spoken at some time before the agreed meeting time.

Can I use your lippie? – This is simple, but might not seem it at first. Usually asked in the female toilets, when a girl wants to add more lipstick and has lost hers. She doesn't have to know the person she's asking, especially if she's drunk too, but it's better to ask a friend. We live in a world of pandemics, remember? If you don't want to lend yours, just pretend you haven't heard.

Jim Jams – Basically a shortened, or lengthier version, of PJ's or pyjamas. 'I'm going to put my jim jams on and go to bed'. Why Jim Jams? Not got a clue, but it is more comforting than pyjamas.

Put a sock in it – Actually nothing whatsoever to do with clothes or wearing socks, but when someone is explaining something and taking a VERY long time about it, just tell them to 'put a sock in it', and they'll stop. It's pretty rude, but they are boring you, so what do you do? No other explanation needed.

Trousers – It's what Americans call pants. Simple really.

Knickers – Female panties. Comes from knickerbockers and was the sole preserve of 1970s British comedians, who only had to say the word for the audience to '**wet their knickers**' with laughter. Whilst we are the topic of knickers, to '**get your knickers in a twist**' is to wind someone up, or get them overly frustrated (often over a practical joke).

Chapter Seven

SAME WORDS, DIFFERENT MEANINGS

"My mind may be American but my heart is British."

T. S. Eliot

On the back of 'pants' or maybe the front, it's time to look at those words that are exactly the same but have totally different meanings. You've probably already silenced a dinner guest by making a comment about a woman's fanny, thinking you were talking about something rather different. So, let's look at the others to save any international incidents. (PS check out chapters 8 & 10 and you'll understand...)

Pants – Yes, we have mentioned this, but pants in the UK also can mean underpants. You know, the things you wear under your pants/trousers?

Jumper – Nope, it's not someone who is about to jump off the Brooklyn Bridge. It's a winter piece of clothing. A pullover, a sweater.

Geezer – Mate or friend here. Very old man in the USA. Could be the same, if you're old too.

Boot – Yes, it's an item of footwear here too, but we also call the empty thing at the back of a car a boot. The place where you throw all your old clothes and kids bikes and garden stuff. Americans call it a trunk.

A car book sale is somewhere you can buy all kinds of **'second-hand'** (used) stuff. You can also find used items in a second-hand shop. You never know, you might actually find something of value. As they say, **'one man's junk is another man's treasure'**.

Rubber – In America this is a condom… our pencil eraser. How can they possibly have become any more different?

First floor – Ground floor in the USA, second floor in the UK. Work that one out.

Chips – Surely the worst difference in the history of English. It's not crisps (you know the stuff you eat out of a packet with a can of Bud), but big fat fries. Fish and Chips.

Oh, for a bit of a history lesson here. '**Fish and chips**' were originally a French idea, and French Fries are Belgian. Maybe don't think too much about this one.

Coach – Becoming a bit more blurred with this one. A coach is a sports team manager, but here it is also a bus. 'I have a coach to catch' is one that'll confuse Americans.

Biscuit – A cookie, not a bread roll.

Post – Not a wooden thing stuck in the ground, but the Royal Mail.

Fag – 'I want a fag' is not something you might hear publicly in the USA, but in Britain it refers to a cigarette. Remember this one next time you go to the pub!

Chapter Eight

TIME. Everyone has time and no time...

The time you enjoy wasting is not wasted time.

Bertrand Russell

Donkey's years – A phrase that has been said incorrectly for...well donkey's years. It's supposed to be donkey's ears, but someone misheard it. It means a very long time, but nobody has a clue as to why.

Fortnight – It seems the Americans rarely use this term. What does it mean? It means FOURTEEN nights, but that is a LOT to say, so we've shortened it to make it easier.

Take your time – He doesn't half take his time...Not sure how you can take your time, but it means don't hurry.

(Actually, it rarely does, as it's now mostly said in a sarcastic manner, so hurry up!)

Fanny around – Okay, so the word fanny has completely different meanings in the USA as to the UK. You may want to refer to chapter ten. Fanny around means that you are wasting someone's time or doing nothing. Guess where it came from? The Royal Navy of course...

Faff around – The same as above. Faff used to mean wind, but now means nothing unless you add the 'around' to it. A more modern term you'll hear a lot is to '**dilly-dally**'. We like that one a lot because it sounds silly.

Have you got the time? – Interesting one, but it normally means you are being asked what time it is, and NOT if you have the time to do something which may be a little less savoury. Don't worry

Chapter Nine

MONEY.

"Saving is a very fine thing. Especially when your parents have done it for you."

Winston Churchill

Ahh money. The root of all evil, and the one thing that no one appears to have enough of. In the UK pounds and pence are still used, as the euro was never accepted, as indeed was belonging to the European Union either...

If you'd arrived in the country at any time before 1970 though, then you'd have to deal with pounds, shillings, pence, farthings and guineas. Even British people couldn't understand it, so be grateful that you're here now!

Money is called all kinds of things in Britain, **wad of notes**, **dough, cash, dosh** and **bread** to name quite a few. Individual amounts get their own slang words. **A quid** is a one-pound coin. **A fiver** is a five-pound note. **A tenner** is a ten-pound note. **A grand** is a thousand pounds, and **loose**

change is the stuff that rattles around in your pockets, and you don't mind giving away or losing.

He's/she's minted – This doesn't mean that he or she has a fondness for mints, but that they've got a lot of money and are able to afford a new car every year. Usually said in a very, very jealous way.

He's/She's loaded – No drug connotation here. It's just the same as above.

He's/She's broke - Exactly the opposite. The word broke comes from bankrupt. '**Going for broke**' has nothing to do with money by the way. It means I'm risking everything to get something…then maybe it has got something to do with money after all.

Knock off – Basically it means that it's a copy of an original but sold at a far cheaper price. Happens regularly in the UK.

SOUNDS LIKE MY SWISS WATCH…
A PIECE OF JUNK I BOUGHT
IN A BACK ALLEY FOR TWENTY QUID.

He could sell ice to an Eskimo – As far as I'm aware no-one has ever tried to do this, and what would be the point anyway? The meaning is that the salesman/woman is so good at their job, that they could literally sell ice to an Eskimo. Try it and see how you get on.

Nick – Yes, it's a name and short for Nicholas, but not here. It means' to steal'. When a UK TV cop grabs a thief, he'll say in a melodramatic way: 'You're nicked sunshine!'.

Old Bill - Named after a cartoon character called Old Bill. Now used to describe the police force, especially in London. Why? They used to sport moustaches that were exactly the same as the character. Not anymore.

A run-in with the old Bill.

So, here are a few tips, should you find yourself in trouble with the Old Bill.

1. They are NOT American cops. They won't point a gun at you unless absolutely necessary.
2. They won't pin you to the ground and shout obscenities at you.
3. They won't then sit in their cars and drink lots of coffee and eat large doughnuts.
4. They WILL talk politely to you.
5. They'll give you a ride in their car and chat about football and things…
6. They'll apologise as they put you in a cell, especially if they aren't really sure why you are there.
7. You'll get lots of tea. If you don't like tea, drink it anyway and try not to offend them.
8. They'll almost certainly let you go and ask if you need a lift anywhere.

What has any of this to do with money? Nothing really, but the word 'bill' fits perfectly!

Like everything, there are those unique British sayings when it comes to the unspeakable. Money.

Chapter Ten.

BEHIND CLOSED DOORS (EXPLICIT!) Anatomy, Toilet-Talk, & Sex.

I want to tell you a terrific story about oral contraception. I asked this girl to sleep with me and she said 'No.'

Woody Allen

The British don't have or do 'sex'. The word doesn't get used that much, or hardly ever. It's the old 'polite' thing again. All the personal stuff is hidden in pubescent words, giggly sentences and sniggering sayings. Try and understand these…

Words for 'toilet' – Toilet can be such a harsh word, so how about **'bog'**, or **'loo'** or **'little boy's room'** (see what I mean?). **'throne'**, **'the crapper'**, **'the gents'** or **'the ladies'**. All used and all mean the same. Oh, WC means Water Closet and not Winston Churchill.

Bog roll – Toilet roll. Not as pleasant though.

Shag – Nothing to do with toilets, but it means sex. Used in a far more politically incorrect time. Hardly heard now. It comes from the 18th century and meant shake. Shake, shag, sex? Me neither.

The Crown Jewels – If you think this refers to our new King, it doesn't. It means a man's genitals. The 'naughty' bits, without referring to them. Like '**float my boat**', it's American from the 1970s, but we use it now, so it's ours.

Meat and two veg – This is definitely ours. Man's genitals. Sausage and sprouts. Get it? Introduced by British soldiers in WW2, but no idea why. It was a difficult time remember?

Bum – Not a drug addicted, alcohol-ridden homeless tramp in New York, but a bottom. Yes, a person's bottom (or ass for Americans), is too nice a word, so it's bum. 'I fell on my bum' has a different meaning to us. It means 'I've fallen over on to my bottom...'

Bell-end – Penis. Do I need to explain? Bell has been used since the 1500s, but bell-end only since 1960. There's actually a village in Worcestershire named after it!

Starkers - Means stark naked, or '**in my birthday suit**'. The second makes sense, but starkers?' Stark literally means barren, so there is some sense to it.

Full Monty – An expression that gave its name to a very successful British film of the 1990s, which you have probably never heard of. It originally meant a three-piece suit, but now it means taking all your clothes off. The film had a lot to do with that…

Fanny – This is going to be fun. Fanny was originally a prostitute who was murdered in 1867. Her 'notoriety' turned the word into slang for a female's genitals. Only the Americans know why it became the buttocks in American English… Oh, how many funny misinterpretations this has brought since. Thank you.

Chapter Eleven

WHEN THINGS GO WRONG...

'The English nation is never so great as in adversity.'

Benjamin Disraeli

We all make a mess of things every now and then, but how we express ourselves is of course totally different on both sides of the pond. If you want to know what a dog's dinner is, or why there's a spanner in the works, then read on.

Cock up – 'balls up', 'screw up' or **'going tits up'** all appear to be strangely British. It means you've done something wrong, like trying to fix a leaking tap and it bursts, or mending a relationship problem, and they leave you. Why the sexual connotation? No idea, but when the great Scots poet Robbie Burns wrote 'Cock up your beaver' it was not misinterpreted as it was well before the playground nature of the English language.

Shambles – It's a mess. Total disorder. Complete confusion. Used to mean slaughterhouse.

A spanner in the works - This originally came from New Zealand, but it's ours now. To throw a 'spanner in the works' of an engine, means it will stop. Used in business, sport, relationships, anything really...

Butchered – Ruined, destroyed, beyond repair.

Botch – If it's a botch job, then it's been done badly. The new roof is cascading water in a shower, and that's a botch job. There is no known origin of this saying, so I think we probably made it up.

Bollocksed it – As above, but usually said by a workman in an angry mood.

Dog's Dinner – If you've made a dog's dinner of something, you've really made a mess of it, BUT it also refers to someone who is dressed in a flashy way. So, 'done up like a dog's dinner' means you look great. That's not confusing at all, is it?

Chapter Twelve

UNUSUAL WORDS OF INSULT

"British humour is very cruel. I love it. It's my favourite kind of humour; if it isn't cruel and funny it doesn't really cut the cake for me."

Elton John

Muppet – 'You muppet!!' It means you're an idiot, and yes, it probably came from the TV programme.

Git – This is so harmless that it's almost funny, but it wasn't always. Originally another word for someone of illegitimate birth – **bastard** – but now is endearing. 'He's a **silly old git**...' The old part is essential.

Tosser – A milder version of **'wanker'**, which isn't a nice thing to say to anyone. 'The referee is a wanker' is one of the most sung chants in English football. Aimed at the type of person who thinks a little too much of themselves.

Slut - Means a female of dubious sexual practices, to make it as polite as possible. In America they might use the word tramp. It's the same really.

What a SLUT.

Sod – Usually used as '**sod off**' which basically means leave, but in an angry way. It replaced **'bugger off'** in people's affections and has the same sodomite type origin. It's mild. Don't be offended.

Minger – Not a nice description at all. Usually describing a female who isn't the greatest looking, or dresses in a rather shabby way. Not to be used at a dinner party.

Pillock – Idiot. Rather quaint now, so if you use it, prepare for giggles and embarrassed looks.

Gormless - Someone who lacks attention or is just plain stupid. Came from the word 'gaum' which means attention. We've modernised it now.

Prat – We Brits love this word. Used as an insult to someone. It means they are seriously stupid. No idea where it came from, but it's a great word.

Chav – A very new and modern way of looking down on the youngsters who try to look 'cool' and wear designer-style sports clothing. Usually sitting around a public playground and selling drugs. Okay, a bit cliche, but they all get 'tarred with the same brush'.

Tarred with the same brush – Not an insult, but I've just mentioned it, so I'd better explain. Actually comes from farmers who would tar their sheep with the same brush, so they didn't lose them. It now means that they all have the same faults.

Plonker - Originally meant penis, but by the late 1970s had become a word associated with an inept person. The British comedy series 'Only Fools and Horses' probably added to its popularity. If you're called a 'plonker', just smile and respond 'Rodney'. You won't understand, but you'll make a friend for life.

Chapter Thirteen

VERY ENGLISH SWEAR WORDS

"The sort of twee person who thinks swearing is in any way a sign of a lack of education or a lack of verbal interest is just a fucking lunatic."

Stephen Fry

Isn't it great when you are being sworn at in a foreign language? Before I learnt the French language, I used to love it when I was insulted with a French word. It sounded so full of charm and didn't feel like I was being sworn at. You may get the same feeling when we British decide to swear at you with some of our words.

Don't dismiss them though, as they really ARE swear words! PS – We're not going to include f@@k, because everyone seems to use that now…

Bloody hell – if you look at the two words on their own, they obviously belong to each other, but what does it mean? It's an exclamation when you are surprised by something.

'Bloody hell, did you see the size of that cow?' The word 'bloody' was always a swear word, but the 'hell' has been added, and no one seems to know why.

Bugger – Obvious what it means but used to be a far more offensive swear word than now. 'Bugger, I've dropped my car keys in the river…' You can also use the term **'bugger off'**, which means go away, but not politely.

Piss off – Okay, we've covered this earlier, but it's just a confirmation that the 'off' makes it into a swear sentence. I know it's confusing…

Whilst we are back again on the topic of piss, **'piece of piss'** means **'easy peasy, lemon squeezy'** (basically, it's very easy).

Damn – 'Damn, damn, damn, **damn you !**' Yep, this is a swear word and expression. From the Middle Ages and a combination of 'harm' and 'damage', so it means they want to hurt you. **'I'll be damned'** is an extension, although not quite as dramatic as it looks. Can also say **'damn it!'**

Shit - We all know it's a swear word, but few know why. There was a suggestion that it was the initials of Ship High in Transit, which referred to vessels in the 17th century that flew the initials on their flag when carrying explosive methane manure. That's turned out to be not true though…

Blimey – Not really a swear word, but more of a cry to God. It comes from 'blind me' and used a century ago when something annoyed you. Saying 'blind me' in today's age, may not be such a good idea.

Blasted - Used by older people. 'This blasted radio keeps crackling…' Now you see what I mean.

Cunt - Possibly the most offensive swear word in the British/English language. Yes, Americans do use it, but nowhere near as harsh as here in old blighty. If someone calls you this, then you're in BIG trouble. Best to back down quickly. It wasn't always offensive though. Regularly used right up to the 20th century, but 'Lady Chatterley's Lover' seemed to redefine the word. Another reason to read the book…

Dickhead – 'You're an idiot.' First used in the 1960s apparently and has never gone away.

Swine – I wish we still used this on a daily basis. If someone calls you a 'swine', they are probably in their 90s and upper class. Comes from 'pig' and describes someone who is at the bottom of the food chain!

Twat – A much gentler way of saying **'cunt'**. It also evolves into **'I twatted him'**, which means someone **'kicked the shit'** out of someone else. Usually spoken in pubs after a few beers.

Knob – As above. **'Knobhead'** is used by Brits to describe those they have absolutely no respect for. Be careful.

Wally – Not a swear word, but a derogatory term for someone who isn't that full of common sense. First used in the 1970s by comedians and is almost a term of affection. Don't be offended. It's almost impossible to be upset by this. Honestly...

Prick – Another version of 'knob' and 'dick'. There are so many different ways of insulting someone by mentioning a penis.

Cow – Not the happy grazing animal, but an offensive term for a woman who is unpopular. You can tone it down by saying '**daft cow**', which is a little nicer, but not by much. '**Stupid cow**' also works.

Big girls' blouse – Ridiculous saying when you read it out loud. It means you are soft. Comes from Lancashire (a county in the north of England) and used extensively on another British TV comedy series 'Nearest and Dearest'. Time for some catch-up 'You Tube' watching, I think.

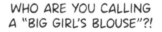

WHO ARE YOU CALLING A "BIG GIRL'S BLOUSE"?!

Tart - Another one from only fools and horses. '**Shut up you tart**'.

Chapter Fourteen.

THE BEST.

"It's a privilege to be in such a great category of people and... I don't believe in God, so I'd like to thank dogs. Dogs have given me everything."

Ricky Gervais

British people are naturally a negative bunch. We like to complain about virtually everything. It's what we are good at. Every now and then though, we are slightly positive, and have a few good things to say. You may be slightly confused with some of the words, but honestly, we are happy when we say them!

Lush – For Americans it means alcohol. For us Brits it means good. If we say something is 'lush', it means it's really nice! A very recent addition to different ways of saying something is okay.

Wicked – The same, except spoken by youngsters. 'I've got tickets for the Bowie-tribute gig on Friday...' 'Wicked!'. Nothing else needed.

The cat's cream – The best, of whatever it is you are describing. Along with **'cat got your tongue?'** and **'there's more than one way to skin a cat'**, shows that we have an unhealthy obsession with our pets.

The cat's whiskers - Okay we seem to have a fixation with cats and what they do and their body parts. It means someone or something that is outstanding. Came from the 1920s, but no one knows why cats were used again!

The dog's bollocks – Exactly the same, except it's a dog. Originally 'it sticks out like a dog's bollocks', but that's far too much to say.

The bee's knees – Now it's a bee. Originally referred to something that didn't exist. Not now though.

Bloody brilliant, blooming marvellous and **absolutely fabulous** are all sayings to prove that we do in fact have good things to say sometimes.

Chapter Fifteen

THE WORST.

"The English are not happy unless they are miserable."

George Orwell

Well obviously, if you have a chapter on the sayings for the best, then we have to have one on the worst!

Rubbish – Garbage in the US, but we say 'rubbish' when something really isn't very good. Your team has just lost 1-0 to a last-minute goal, and the kinder expression would be 'that was rubbish'…there are stronger ones!

(Also, its worth nothing that we say 'rubbish bin' instead of 'trash can'.)

Crap – This is a gentler word than shit. Whereas shit is definitely obscene, crap is kinder and almost funny.

Load of tosh – A rather upper-class way of saying '**what a load of old rubbish!**' It's mostly used to call someone out on something someone has just told you (ie – you're lying), or just something that has happened. The explanation to the origin of this expression is so complex, that I decided it was just 'a load of tosh!'.

Utter nonsense – When you don't believe a single word the other person has just said, then this is the response. It's just about the most withering response, and very difficult to come back from!

Literally unbelievable – Used by youngsters when something they are surprised by has confused them. To be literally unbelievable means that you just will not be able to believe it, but that's far too complicated.

Second rate - Another navy term. Described the size of a galleon in the 17th century, but now refers to something that is sub-standard. If you're described this way, be very offended!

The literal worst - Used to describe something that you want to exaggerate as being just about the worst thing that has ever happened to you…

According to Buzzfeed.com, the TEN literal worst things to experience during your day are:

1. Receiving a voicemail
2. Packing (PS - I agree!)
3. Waiting in a queue in a Post Office (that's waiting in a line to the Americans reading this…)
4. Burning your tongue on a hot drink. Ouch!
5. People who eat your food from the office fridge. (Granted, those people are the literal worst…)
6. Stepping on a piece of 'Lego'!
7. People who go to work when they are sick (or to make this covid relevant, those who wear their masks under their noses…)
8. Moving house - yep
9. Taking a pill and not being sure if it has gone down your throat. Literally the worst.
10. People who misuse of the word 'literally'. Uh oh.

This list kinda puts 'first world problems' into perspective, don't ya think?

Chapter Sixteen.

TV & FILM you MUST see before attempting any British slang

"I don't want to talk to you no more, you empty-headed animal food trough wiper. I fart in your general direction. Your mother was a hamster and your father smelt of elderberries."

French knight to King Arthur, Monty Python and the Holy Grail

You've read all the slang sayings and the crazy catchwords that we use here, so now you're ready to take on the British/English language? Not so fast...Watch a few moments of English brilliance before trying to ingratiate yourselves with us. We speak the 'King's English', not an American drawl. Watch and learn...We'll start with a few films.

1) **The Long Good Friday** – This 1980 British gangster film, starring Bob Hoskins at the beginning of his career, has become a cult watch. Unfortunately, the Americans couldn't understand a single word that our Bob had to say,

because he spoke 'Cockney' Simple. Get it dubbed. So, what did they do? They dubbed it into a Wolverhampton accent, which no-one in Britain, outside of that place, can understand anyway!

2) **Zulu** – Not for the fact that around 100 British soldiers managed to take on a few thousand Zulu warriors and won (it's a loosely-based tale on fact), but the high-ranking officer and upper-class accent of Michael Caine. It's brilliant! Pause the film and try to repeat the words. I bet you can't.

3) **This Happy Breed** – Set between the two world wars. Brilliant film, but YES, we actually did talk like that!

4) **Dunkirk** – Despite a cast of thousands, hardly a word spoken throughout the film. It shows that we value what we say. Say little and mean more.

"I'VE FUSED 'FLASHDANCE'...
WITH MC HAMMER SH!T."

David Brent from 'The Office' (a must-watch)

Now for the television, which won't take anywhere near as much of your time.

1) **EastEnders** – A long running soap-opera set in some fictional area of London. No one likes each other, and it's the kind of place where people just disappear, and nobody seems to care. Watch an episode and listen to the accents. They do talk that way in London...

2) **Last of the Summer Wine** – If you want to listen to northern English slang, then this is the programme for you. You probably won't understand a word of it, but then neither did most of the British audience. The longest running comedy series in the history of British television, which was a remarkable achievement, bearing in mind it was never actually funny.

3) **Only Fools and Horses** – If you STILL don't understand the meaning of the word '**plonker**', then watch this. An absolute gem.

4) **Dr Who** – As virtually every episode of this is set in Britain, you'll hear a variety of accents and understand a lot of slang sayings.

5) **Rab Nesbitt** – If you venture north of Hadrian's Wall and enter Scotland, it's essential you watch this first, otherwise you will have no idea what people are saying.

6) **Game of Thrones** - As if no one has seen this? Full of British actors and accents, mainly because they sound more believable when dealing with dragons and castles and weird sex. 'Winter is Coming' stolen by British politicians when warning that the government's policies just might not work.

7) **The Crown** - The fictional account of a family who are Royal in the United Kingdom. Any passing similarity to our own Royal Family is purely coincidental.

8) **Peaky Blinders** - If you want to listen to a variety of versions of the Birmingham accent, then this is for you. Based on a real life 'Peaky Blinders' gang at the beginning of the last century, who had nothing like the glamour of Cillian Murphy.

9) **Downton Abbey** - Just about the most popular British programme watched by Americans I assume. Yes, we do all live like this, and yes we are all very fond of our servants who seem to go from one crisis to another. The accents are real and not in any way whatsoever exaggerated for entertainment purposes.

10) **Sherlock** - Obviously you don't have to read numerous novels of the famous detective from a century ago. Listen to the accents, especially the character played by Una Stubbs. Yes, landladies like that really DO exist here.

Chapter Seventeen.

COCKNEY SLANG

I'm every bourgeois nightmare - a Cockney with intelligence and a million dollars.

Michael Caine

I've saved this until nearly the last. It's mainly because most American tourists spend their time in our capital city, and so convince themselves that the whole of the UK talk this way. Well, not really. Even in London, there are so many different accents and of course, slangs.

Being 'Cockney' means that you were born in the East End of London, or within earshot of the '**Bow Bells**' (that's a church by the way, but far too much to explain), and so a certain way of speaking comes with that honour.

Do they actually speak this way? The answer is yes...Read these and understand, but under no circumstances must you try to use these sayings yourself when you are anywhere near London. It won't work with an American accent. Just think of

Dick van Dyke in 'Mary Poppins' and you'll understand why... Remember, it has to rhyme, or it doesn't work.

Adam and Eve – Believe (see, it rhymes...!)

Alan Whicker's – Knickers. Alan Whicker was a TV personality of many years ago. Knickers are...return to chapter six to check.

Artful Dodger – Lodger

Apples and pears – Stairs

Ascot Races – Braces. They were used to hold up trousers, well before the invention of a belt!

Aunt Joanna – Piano – it's pronounced 'pianna' in case you're a bit confused.

Baker's Dozen – Cousin. A 'baker's dozen' is actually 13. You don't need to know why.

Ball and Chalk – Walk

Barnaby Rudge – Judge

Barnet Fair – Hair

Barney Rubble – Trouble

Battlecruiser – Boozer. This is another word for pub. Forgot to mention it earlier.

Bees and honey – Money

Boat Race – Face. The Boat Race is held on the Thames between the universities of Oxford and Cambridge every year. Despite the fact that both crews now seem to be made up of Americans, the whole nation is absorbed in it.

OXFORD WON THE BOAT RACE?!
WHO CAME IN SECOND?

Bob Hope – Soap. Bob Hope was British by the way.

Bottle and glass – Arse. The glass is pronounced glares.

Brahms and Liszt – Pissed (drunk). Pissed has made more appearances in this book then virtually any other word.

Brass Tacks – Facts

Bread and Cheese – Sneeze

Bread and Honey – Money

Bricks and Mortar – Daughter

Bristol City – Breasts. Okay, this is really confusing. It's the name of a football team, but Bristols can refer to breasts, and City rhymes with tittie…Get it?

Brown Bread – Dead. You'd prefer to hear Brown Bread than Dead, wouldn't you?

Bubble and Squeak – Greek. Bubble and Squeak is a mashed potato and cabbage meal that is a lot nicer than it sounds. Only available in the East End!

Bubble Bath – Laugh

Butcher's hook – A look

Chalk Farm – Arm

China plate – Mate. You know what mate is now…

Cock and Hen – Ten

Cows and Kisses – Missus (wife)

Custard and jelly – Telly (television)

Daisy Roots – Boots

Darby and Joan – Moan. Used frequently.

Dicky Bird – Word. Dicky Bird was also a cricket umpire, which just adds to the mystery.

Dicky Dirt – Shirt

Dog and bone – Phone. The equipment that Americans NEVER say 'goodbye' into after speaking.

Duck and Dive – Skive. When you disappear from work or school. Another way of saying it is to **bunk off**, or do a **no show**.

Duke of Kent – Rent

Dustbin lid – Kid. Dustbin is a garbage holder, and kid is a child…

Elephant's Trunk – Drunk. Saying Elephant's Trunk when you are drunk is an achievement.

Fireman's Hose – Nose

Frog and Toad – Road

Gypsy's kiss – Piss. This version of our favourite word means to urinate.

Half-inch – Pinch (to steal)

Hampton Wick – Prick. We covered '**prick**' already on page 55.

Hank Marvin – Starving

Irish pig – Wig

Jam-jar – Car. Jam is jelly to Americans. Jelly is something different to us.

Jimmy Riddle – Piddle. Urinate. Piss….

Kick and Prance – Dance

Lady Godiva – Fiver

Laugh n a joke – Smoke. But not the smoke you're now thinking of… Another version of 'smoke' is the centre of London, when it was very smoky due to pollution. It's clean now, but we still like to call it 'The Smoke'.

Lionel Blair's – Flares. Lionel Blair was a dancing comedian from years ago. Flares were trousers from the 1970s. Still used though.

Loaf of Bread – Head

Mickey Bliss – Piss…again.

Mince Pies – Eyes. Mince pies are a traditional cake for Christmas. There is NO mince in them though, as Rachel found out in 'Friends'.

Mork and Mindy – Windy. Also a famous American TV series of course.

North and south – Mouth

Orchestra stalls – Balls

Pat and Mick – Sick

Plates of meat – Feet

Pony and Trap – Crap. We explained this word already in chapter thirteen).

Raspberry ripple – Nipple. Raspberry ripple is a classic ice-cream.

Raspberry tart – Fart. Passing wind…gas etc

Roast Pork – Fork

Rosy Lee – Tea

Rub-a-Dub – Pub. We have a LOT of names for the pub.

Ruby Murray – Curry

Sausage Roll – Goal

Septic tank – Yank. For all the Americans reading this…

Skin and Blister – Sister

Sky Rocket – Pocket

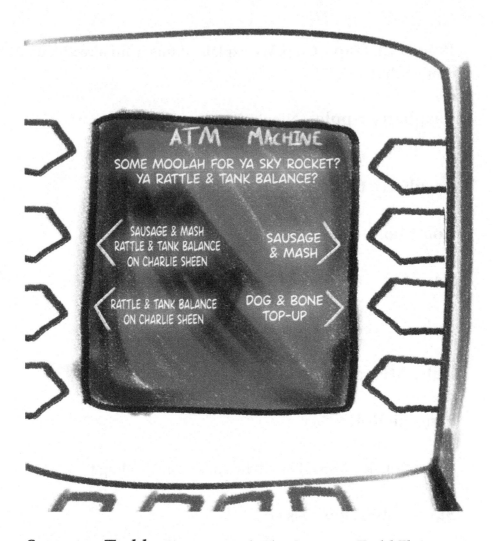

Sweeney Todd – Flying squad. The Sweeney Todd Flying Squad does exist in the police force.

Tables and chairs – Stairs

Tea leaf – Thief

Tom and Dick – Sick

Tomfoolery – Jewellery

Tommy Trinder – Window. Tommy Trinder was a very popular London comedian from absolutely ages ago. Still used every day.

Trouble and strife – Wife

Two and eight – State (of upset and not the union)

Vera Lynn – Gin

Whistle and flute – Suit (of clothes)

Wonga – Cash. Doesn't rhyme, but the infamous loan company has taken over the word of cash, mainly because none of us have it anymore. We're all on the Wonga!

Chapter Eighteen.

BITS & BOBS. Other stuff that doesn't fit anywhere else...

"If an earthquake were to engulf England tomorrow, the English would manage to meet and dine somewhere among the rubble, just to celebrate the event."

Douglas Jerrold

In this final chapter, we'll throw a few odd phrases at you that you may be confused by (well you WILL be confused by). They don't belong to any group, so they're here instead!

A Penny for your thoughts - If someone offered me a penny for my thoughts today, I'd keep quiet, but it meant a lot more in 1535 when Thomas More wrote it in a novel. If someone asks and you tell them, don't expect to be paid.

Back to square one - It means to start again. First used in BBC radio football commentaries in the 1930s. To help the listener, the Radio Times (a BBC listings magazine) printed a football pitch divided into squares. Square one was the goalmouth. I used to commentate, and NO I didn't use it in 1930.

An Arm and a Leg - Means to cost more than expected. It referred to the price of paintings and used as 'I'd give an arm and a leg to buy it' . First started in the 1940s, and was used a lot in America, but it's ours now.

Barking up the wrong tree – It was originally used when hunting. A dog, who had cornered its prey up a tree, would bark for its owner. If it was dark though, it would mistake the tree! Today it means, you're wrong, or you've made a mistake!

Beat about the bush - 15th century saying for those who used to beat bushes to scare the birds who would then subsequently get shot. Now it means that you aren't getting to the point. There really isn't an explanation as to why.

Best thing since sliced bread - The invention of sliced bread was as important as the invention of the wheel for the British. Now you could buy bread that you didn't have to slice! Can you imagine? The 1930s were a wonderful time.

Don't give up your day job - It means that no matter how good you think you are, you're actually not. So, if you have employment, stick with it.

I don't give a monkeys' - It means you don't care about something. **I couldn't care less** - or more if you are from the USA. No record of origin, or what part of the monkey's anatomy it refers to…

Hit the nail on the head - Came from carpentry (obviously) and means that you have got something EXACTLY right. Why? Pretty self-explanatory, you've got it **spot on**.

Speak of the Devil - You're talking about someone, and they suddenly turn up. It was first used in the 16th century when people were reminded NOT to speak of the devil. Seems to have changed its meaning now.

About as useful as a chocolate teapot – Unless you've ever actually tried making a teapot out of chocolate, I can't imagine it would go too well… This hilarious saying is used to describe someone or something as completely and utterly useless!

Look after the pennies and the pounds will look after themselves - Could and should be in the money section, but nice to put it here.. Pretty obvious what it means, and first used in the 18th century. A father wrote it to his child, and then it became famous!!

Kill two birds with one stone - It means to complete two tasks at the same time, such as dropping the children off at school whilst on your way to work. Again, no known origins, although killing two birds with one stone would be an achievement

Chapter Nineteen

CONCLUSION

"Death is too negative for me. So I'll be popping off for a long cup of tea. Do splash out on two bags in the pot. And for god's sake, keep the water hot."

Michael Ashby

That's it. You know the slang. You know the words. You know how to speak British. You should be able to go to a pub and order two pints of lager and a packet of crisps, and not be laughed at.

You can go to Stamford Bridge (it's a football ground and not a bridge by the way) and shout 'You're a wanker' at the ref, and know what you mean.

Basically you can speak British English, even with an American accent. Now get out there and embarrass yourself!

A quick note about the contents of this book:

Every effort has been made to ensure that the slang phrases, words and expressions mentioned in this book are as accurate and up to date as possible. Granted, I could have written a textbook of slang terms that's longer than my list of ex-girlfriends, but I'd have lost you at page one.

Instead, what this book provides is a simple guide to how people actually speak in Britain today (we'll just gloss over the cockney slang…) Yes, we could have included all the cliché idioms you see in ESL textbooks, but truth is, no one barely uses them in real life (unless we've included them in this book).

But most of all, we hope you've had a good ol' laugh at some of the ridiculous phrases used in old blighty. I've certainly had a blast writing it! And many thanks to the amazing Sam Davies who worked his magic with the illustrations for this book, many of which left me in stitches.

If you've enjoyed this book, then one very good way to show your support and appreciation is to **kindly leave us a review on Amazon**. We really do appreciate all of your feedback and nice comments. It helps us out immensely. Thank you!

Alternatively, if you wish to see something added to this book, or you've spotted a mistake, please email me using my email address below:

jeffwatson688@gmail.com

Chapter Twenty

A Nifty Little Glossary of Slang Terms

"There's an accent shift, on average, every 25 miles in England"

David Crystal

Nifty – a useful trick, thing or ability. For example, "check out my really nifty little travel case for my headphones", or "I discovered a nifty trick to open a beer with a lighter".

Got a slang term on the tip of your tongue but can't quite remember the meaning?

Lucky for you, I've compiled a handy list of every single slang term/expression in this whole book, so you can flip to the page it is mentioned and jog your memory about its meaning.

Enjoy!

Made in United States
North Haven, CT
06 August 2024

55733742R00059